CUT & COLLAGE

Mushrooms & Fungi

*Magnificent Images
from the Forest Floor*

EARTH AWARE

SAN RAFAEL LOS ANGELES LONDON

INTRODUCTION

Collage, from the French coller, meaning "to glue" or "to stick together," is an art form with endless possibilities that dates back as early as 200 BC. A collage is created by piecing together different overlapping materials, such as photographs or paper, to create something new. Collage is a tactile art form, where the act of cutting and arranging materials becomes a meditative practice—a unique blend of textures, colors, and shapes that captivates the senses.

Filled with hundreds of vibrant, eye-catching images ready to be cut out, this book is your trusty companion for collage art. *Cut & Collage Mushrooms and Fungi* invites you to piece together your own creations inspired by the treasures found on the forest floor.

The stunning images in this book offer inspiration for all your crafting projects, from collages and vision boards to scrapbooks, handmade cards, and school projects. Let your creativity and imagination roam free as you mix and match vibrant colors, textures, and inspirational quotes. In the pages ahead you'll find captivating photographs and illustrations that celebrate the beauty and magic of the fungus kingdom, including macro photography of oyster, portobello, glowing bioluminescent mushrooms, and more. Images highlight the biodiversity of the forest floor, capturing woodland creatures including snails, frogs, rabbits, and more.

As you delve in, keep in mind that collage art is a wonderfully liberating process because it allows for boundless creativity and interpretation. There is no right or wrong way to create a collage. Let yourself be inspired, find what works for you, and remember to have fun in the process.

HERE ARE SOME IDEAS TO HELP YOU GET STARTED:

CHOOSE A THEME

You may want to choose a specific subject you find interesting to focus your collage around. It could be a mushroom species like the portobello mushroom or a woodland creature such as the poison dart frog.

EXPERIMENT WITH COMPOSITION

Play with different arrangements of your materials. Try a few different placements before gluing. Cut shapes, tear edges, and layer pieces over one another to create depth and visual interest.

TELL A STORY

Use collage to convey a narrative or evoke a specific mood. Consider how colors, textures, and spatial relationships can communicate the feeling of being immersed in nature's beauty.

CRAFT A VISION BOARD

A vision board is a collection of images and words that embody your goals and inspire you to reach them. Think on the person that you'd like to become, your short and long-term goals, and the places you'd like to visit one day. Express these ideals, emotions, and hopes in your vision board.

CREATE A MOSAIC COLLAGE

You can make a mosaic collage by assembling small cut-outs in various colors into a larger image or pattern of your choosing, such as a mushroom, flower, tree, or even a person. Collect cut-outs in the colors needed and piece them together to create your vision.

EXPLORE MIXED MEDIA

Don't limit yourself! While you have everything you need in this book, you may want to gather additional inspirational materials to add to your artwork. You can incorporate personal ephemera, fabrics, magazine clippings, and even three-dimensional objects like pressed flowers and leaves to add a tactile dimension to your art and evoke the essence of nature.

EMBRACE SPONTANEITY

Lastly, you can absolutely go in with no specific vision or process in mind. Flip through the pages in this book and find what images you're drawn to, cut them out, and let your creativity guide the way.

As you channel your inner artist and cut, layer, and arrange elements to build your own unique creations, you'll find yourself connecting with the beauty of fungi in a uniquely personal way. So grab your scissors, unleash your creativity, and get ready to lose yourself in the art of collage.

ENJOY EVERY MOMENT

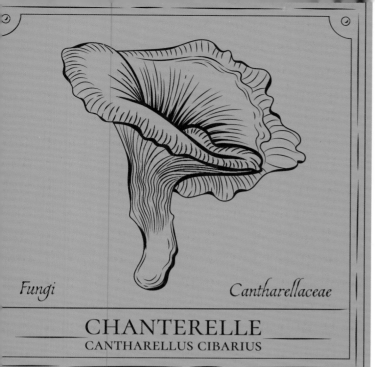

Fungi   *Cantharellaceae*

CHANTERELLE
CANTHARELLUS CIBARIUS

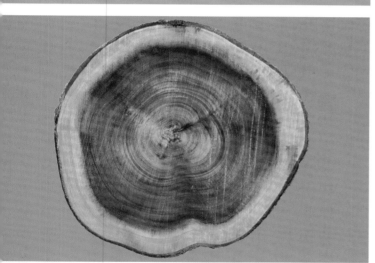

Be Wild and free

STAY POSITIVE AND HAPPY

YOU WILL FIND ME IN THE FOREST

NATURE
IS MY
Happy
PLACE

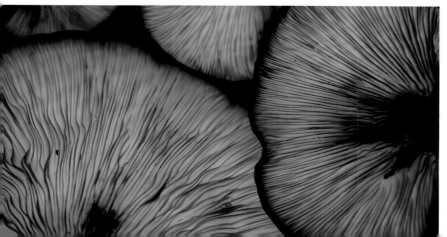

CHOOSE HAPPY

Fungi

Russulaceae

RED PINE MUSHROOM
LACTARIUS DELICIOSUS

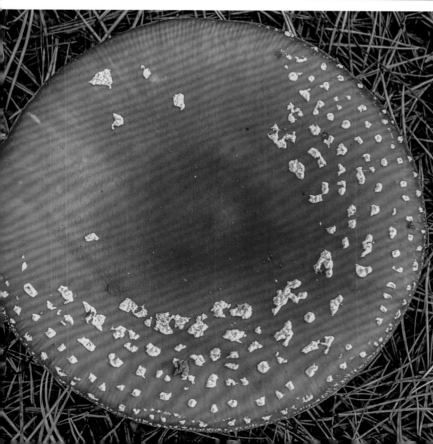

Bloom & grow

grow positive thoughts

Doing my best

LET THE SUNSHINE IN

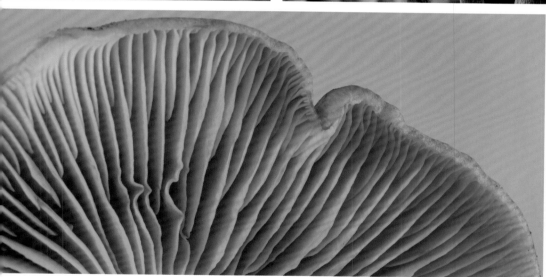

Fungi

Amanitaceae

FLY AGARIC
AMANITA MUSCARIA

ORGANIC PRODUCT

PREMIUM QUALITY

ES TD

20 24

MUSHROOM

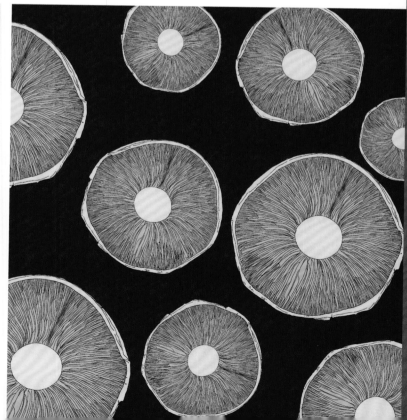

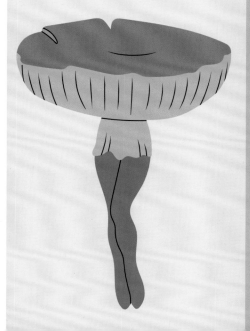

keep
NATURE
wild

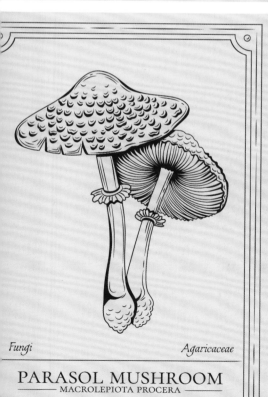

Fungi   *Agaricaceae*

PARASOL MUSHROOM
MACROLEPIOTA PROCERA

ENJOY NATURE

NEVER GIVE UP

Enjoy the little THINGS

Stay groovy

STEP inside NATURE

Free Spirit

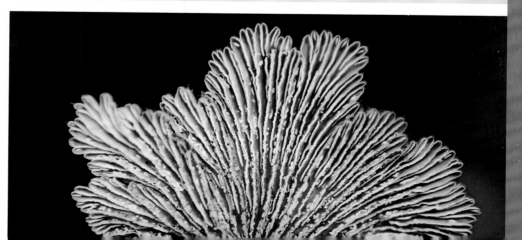

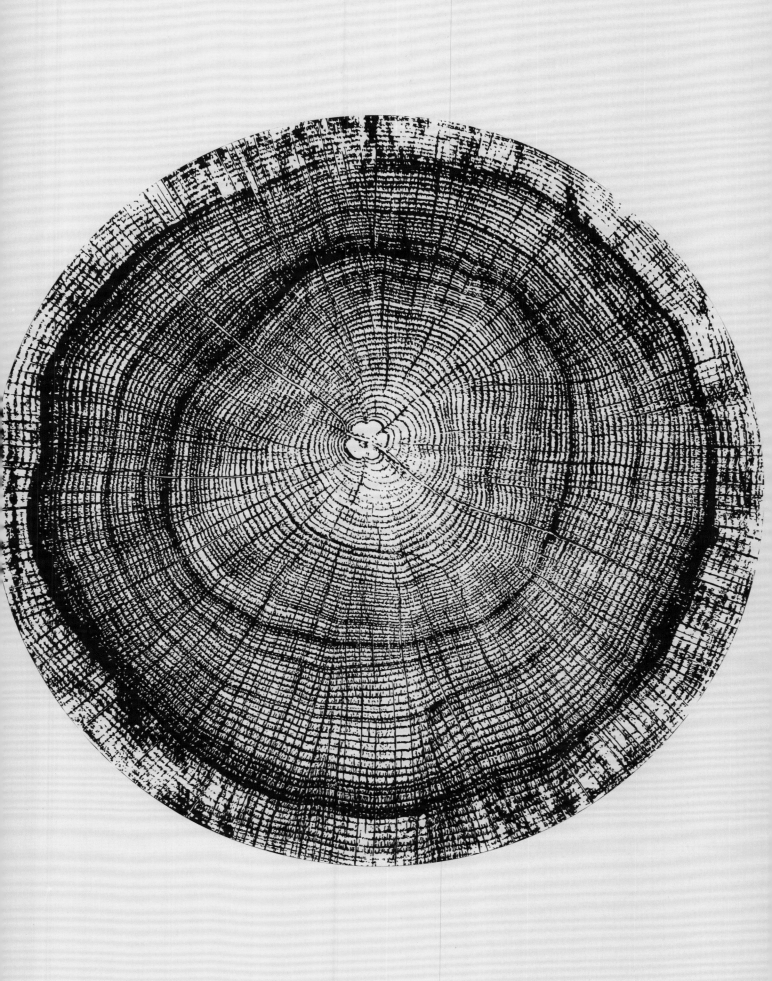

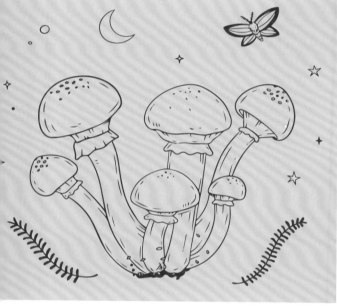

Wild
&
Free

GET BACK TO
NATURE
to find
YOURSELF

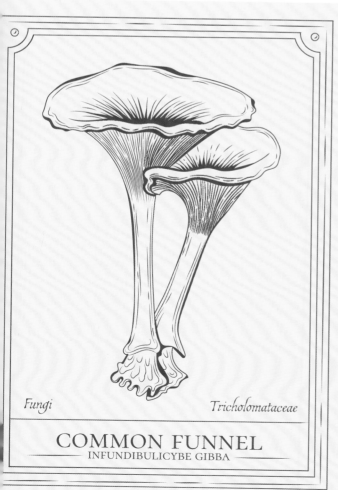

Fungi   *Tricholomataceae*

COMMON FUNNEL
INFUNDIBULICYBE GIBBA

EARTH AWARE

An Imprint of MandalaEarth
PO Box 3088
San Rafael, CA 94912
mandalaearth.com

Find us on Facebook: www.facebook.com/mandalaearth

Publisher Raoul Goff
Associate Publisher Roger Shaw
Publishing Director Katie Killebrew
Editor Peter Adrian Behravesh
Assistant Editor Amanda Nelson
VP Creative Chrissy Kwasnik
Creative Director Ashley Quackenbush
Senior Designer Stephanie Odeh
VP Manufacturing Alix Nicholaeff
Production Associate Tiffani Patterson
Sr Production Manager, Subsidiary Rights Lina s Palma-Temena

Cover design by Faceout Studio, Molly von Borstel

ISBN: 979-8-88762-148-7

Manufactured in China by Insight Editions
10 9 8 7 6 5 4 3 2 1

ROOTS of PEACE   REPLANTED PAPER

Insight Editions, in association with Roots of Peace, will plant two trees for each tree used in the manufacturing of this book. Roots of Peace is an internationally renowned humanitarian organization dedicated to eradicating land mines worldwide and converting war-torn lands into productive farms and wildlife habitats. Roots of Peace will plant two million fruit and nut trees in Afghanistan and provide farmers there with the skills and support necessary for sustainable land use.

FSC
www.fsc.org
MIX
Paper | Supporting
responsible forestry
FSC® C188448